Christmas Charcuterie Board

Delicious and Unique Recipes for Your Holiday Party

Contents

INTRODUCTION

The holiday season is upon us, and you might be wondering what kind of treats and snacks you can set out for your guests to keep them busy (and satisfied) while you're putting the finishing touches on the main course.

Consider these Christmas charcuterie board ideas; there's something here for everyone. Traditionally, these boards are made of savory cured meats, artisan cheeses, crackers, fruits, and an assortment of jams and honey.

You're not limited to just those standards. You can branch out, incorporating desserts, veggies, or combinations of new and old ideas.

It's the holiday season and the time to be merry! Be adventurous and try something new that impresses your guests and leaves you satisfied with your hosting abilities.

Christmas Tree Charcuterie Board

This Christmas Tree Charcuterie Board will be a showstopper at your Christmas gathering! This easy charcuterie board is a great way to kick off the holiday season and impress your friends and family. Follow these simple step-by-step instructions and you'll be surprised how easy it is!

Prep Time:45 mins
Total Time:45 mins
Servings: 10 Calories: 443kcal

INGREDIENTS

- 8 oz. fontina Cheese, cubed see other cheese options below
- 8 oz. smoked Gouda, cubed see other cheese options below
- 9 oz. genoa salami, cubed see other meat options below
- 6 oz pepperoni see other meat options below
- 1/2 cup green olives
- 1/4 cup dried cranberries
- 1/4 cup almonds
- 3-4 tbsp honey mustard or Delicatessen style mustard
- 1 5 oz rosemary flatbread crackers see other cracker options below
- 1 4.25 oz water crackers see other cracker options below

- fresh pomegranate seeds for garnish see other garnish options below
- 8-10 rosemary sprigs for your "tree branches"

NOTES

*Starred items are exact items I used in this charcuterie board.

Meat Options
- Prosciutto
- *Salami
- Sopressata
- *Pepperoni
- Capocollo
- Mortadella
- Deli meats (ham, turkey, etc.)

Cheese Options
- Brie
- Cheddar cheese cubes
- Parmigiano Reggiano
- Manchego
- Mozzarella balls (plain or marinated)
- Gouda
- Fontina

Dips and Spreads
- Hummus
- Jams & Jellies

- *Honey Mustard
- Pesto
- Honey
- Spinach Dip
- Ranch Dressing

Bread/Crackers

- *Water Crackers
- Whole Wheat Crackers
- *Flavored Crackers such as rosemary
- French bread/baguette
- Pretzel sicks
- Bread sticks
- Pita chips/pita bread

Extras/Garnishes

- *Rosemary sprigs
- Pickles
- *Olives
- *Nuts
- *Dried Cranberries
- Fresh pomegranate seeds
- Cherry tomatoes
- Cucumber
- Grapes
- Cherries
- Chocolate

INSTRUCTIONS

- Start at the base of your tree with your meats and cheeses. Make one layer that goes almost the width of the board. Make each "layer" slightly shorter than the next. Remember to leave room at the bottom for your "tree trunk."
- The cute little pepperoni layer was done by just folding the pepperoni slices into quarters and sticking them onto toothpicks. So easy!
- Next, layer your smaller items or "extras" such a nuts, olives, dried fruit, grapes, etc.
- Place rosemary stems between your layers for the Christmas tree look.
- Last, place any dips and spreads you are using around your board. I used honey mustard in a small white ramekin for the "trunk" of my tree. Also, add bread and crackers around the board. "Decorate" the tree with red pomegranate seeds for another splash of color!
- Use a star cookie cutter (or freehand it with a sharp knife) to cut a star shape from a slice of cheese for the top of the tree.
- Note: For best results, allow items to come to room temperature for 15-30 minutes before serving. OR wrap the board tightly with several layers of plastic wrap and store in the fridge for up to 12 hours.

Nutrition information is approximate based on the Very Well Fit nutrition calculator. Does not include crackers, bread and other condiments.

NUTRITION

Calories: 443kcal | Carbohydrates: 2g | Protein: 24g | Fat: 37g | Saturated Fat: 18g | Cholesterol: 103mg | Sodium: 1562mg | Potassium: 165mg | Fiber: 0.5g | Sugar: 1g | Vitamin D: 17µg | Calcium: 321mg | Iron: 1mg

Christmas Wreath Cheese Board

Looking for impressive yet easy appetizers for the Holidays? Why not make this Christmas wreath cheese board! This fun cheese platter is easily customizable!

PREP TIME: 20 minutes
TOTAL TIME: 20 minutes

YIELD: 8 SERVING
SIZE: 1

INGREDIENTS

- Fresh Rosemary Sprigs, see note 1
- 14 Mini Mozzarella Balls
- Prosciutto, torn into bite-size pieces
- 14 Cherry Tomatoes
- 4 ounces Red Cheddar Cheese, diced (120 grams)
- ¼ English Cucumber, sliced
- 1 cup Grapes
- 1 cup Olives
- Fresh Cranberries
- ¼ teaspoon Dried Oregano

INSTRUCTIONS

- Start by forming a large circle out of the rosemary sprigs: Either you put them onto a large round cheese board/tray/plate loosely and form a circle out of them or you tie them together with a wire first(I used a wire for sugar flowers – this is used in cake making) and then shape them into a circle.
- Once done, you can start arranging everything around the wreath. I started with Caprese bites (on a cocktail stick, thread cherry tomato, a piece of prosciutto or basil and mini mozzarella ball). Make 14 and arrange them around.
- Next, arrange the rest of the ingredients and fill any gaps with cranberries.
- You can also sprinkle the ready-made wreath with dried oregano or thyme, if you like.
- This wreath is best served within 2-3 hours.

NUTRITION INFORMATION:

Amount Per Serving: CALORIES: 255
- TOTAL FAT: 18g
- SATURATED FAT: 10g
- TRANS FAT: 0g
- UNSATURATED FAT: 7g
- CHOLESTEROL: 54mg
- SODIUM: 578mg
- CARBOHYDRATES: 9g
- FIBER: 2g
- SUGAR: 5g
- PROTEIN: 15g

Christmas Charcuterie Board

Prep Time: 10 minutes
Total Time: 30 minutes
Calories: 1000kcal

Ingredients

- Block of sharp white cheddar
- Triple Cream Brie
- Block of aged manchego
- Package of charcuterie meats
- Fig & Olive crisp crackers
- Box of assorted crackers
- Red beet crackers
- Truffle or smoked almonds
- Green olives
- Red and green bell peppers
- Cucumber
- Pesto for dipping
- Raspberries
- Pomegranate
- Red grapes
- Green pear
- Dried cranberries or cherries
- Dried Fuji apples
- Peppermint Meringues
- Fig preserves
- Fresh rosemary

INSTRUCTIONS

Prep your ingredients on a separate cutting board. Unbox crackers.

Cube the cheddar. Slice the manchego in triangles and stack vertically. Once you have a tower, you can turn on its side to be seen as zig zags on the board.

Roll the longer meats into cigars. Fold circle meats into "flowers" by folding in half and folding in half again. Wash and slice fruits and vegetables into thin slices or strips. Pour vegetable dip into a little bowl

Arrange cheeses evenly across the board.

Add meats in curved line around cheeses, arranging the longer rolls as vertical as possible

Arrange bowls of dip and olives
Add fruits and vegetables all around board
Decorate with crackers in stacks and rows
Fill in edges and holes with nuts, dried fruit and herbs
Top brie with preserves and meringues on top!

If you're taking your board outside or need a germ-safe way to share this, consider mini to-go containers like this Picnic Charcuterie Board. Just divide up and pack everything inside of a holiday themed to go box (like these) or holiday tin and enjoy one per family. Leave a cheese board on your friends' doorsteps instead of cookies this year!

Christmas Dessert Charcuterie Board

PREP TIME: 15minutes mins
TOTAL TIME: 15minutes mins
SERVINGS: 15 people

INGREDIENTS

- 2 Candy Canes
- 4 Chocolate Covered Pretzel Sticks
- 4 Pirouettes
- 4 Snowman Marshmallows
- 1 cup Christmas M&M's
- 4 Stroopwafels
- 1 cup Cinnamon Bears
- 2 cup Mini Vanilla Wafers
- 2 cups Peppermint Marshmallows
- 5 Snowflake Marshmallows
- 2 Little Debbie Christmas Tree Cakes
- 1 cup Soft Peppermint Candies
- 2 cups Peppermint Popcorn
- 1 cup Peppermint Hershey Kisses
- 2 cups Mini Peanut Butter Sandwich Crackers
- 2 cups Mini Chocolate Chip Cookies
- 1 cup Mini Pink & Red Starbursts
- 5 Reese's Christmas Trees
- 4 Ghirardelli Chocolate Snowmen
- 2 cups Mini Fudge Stripes Cookies
- 7 Chocolate Bells
- 3 Candy Sour Strips

INSTRUCTIONS

- First, grab the board, platter, or dish that you'd like to use. If you're wanting to buy the large wooden board that I used here, this is where you can get this charcuterie board.
- Next, what I love to do is put the bigger items on the board first. If serving a dip (like this Christmas Tree Cake Dip) I like to put that in the center of the board and then place items around it. However, with this board, I didn't have a dip but I used the Christmas Tree Cakes as the center of attention.
- Then, I start putting other big items (large marshmallows, chocolate-covered pretzels, and candy canes) in the corners. (Mainly because the big items can overlap and hang over the edge of the board to allow more room for smaller items on the board.
- Then, I start picking out the smaller items (but not the smallest... you'll see why in the next step.) and start placing them from the outside of the board, and work my way in toward the center.
- Finally, I take the smallest items, like M&M's, and fill in the gaps where I can see the board.

NOTES

Storage:
If you happen to have leftover items, store them in their original containers (I usually save them and hide them in the pantry in case I need them again) or in plastic bags or in Tupperware.

NUTRITION

Serving: 0.25cup | Calories: 971kcal | Carbohydrates: 148g | Protein: 10g | Fat: 40g | Saturated Fat: 18g | Polyunsaturated Fat: 8g | Monounsaturated Fat: 9g | Trans Fat: 0.3g | Cholesterol: 9mg | Sodium: 458mg | Potassium: 202mg | Fiber: 4g | Sugar: 89g | Vitamin A: 72IU | Vitamin C: 9mg | Calcium: 81mg | Iron: 3mg

Candy Cane Christmas Charcuterie Board

Ingredients

- 2 ounces white cheddar, sliced (about ½ cup)
- 1 pepperoni link, sliced into disks
- 4 ounces goat cheese, roughly crumbled
- ½ cup fresh raspberries
- 1 cup white chocolate covered pretzels
- ½ cup sugared or dried cranberries
- 2 ounces Monterey jack cheese, cubed (about ½ cup)
- 1 ounce dry salami (about 8 slices)
- 4 ounces cherry 'ciliegine' size mozzarella balls (about ½ cup)
- Fresh rosemary sprigs for decorating

Instructions

Start by arranging a 2" row of sliced white cheddar cheese in the lower right corner of a medium sized serving platter or board.

Add a row of sliced pepperoni immediately above the white cheddar. Repeat with goat cheese and raspberries.

Add the pretzels above the raspberries creating a slight curve towards the left in the top of the row to start the top of the "candy cane".

Add the cranberries next to the pretzels to create the very top of the candy cane. The cranberries should be at the top center of your board.

Add the cubed Monterey jack cheese next to the cranberries curving the opposite way of the pretzels to complete the top and start the smaller side of the candy cane.

Fold your salami and add next to the Monterey Jack cheese. Finally, add the mozzarella balls to finish up the candy cane shape.

Add small sprigs of rosemary as a festive garnish throughout.

Notes

- This candy cane board is best made right before it will be served to help keep the various cheeses from drying out and the mozzarella from creating puddles on the board.
- The charcuterie board can be left out at room temperature for up to two hours. After that it is best to package up and refrigerate any leftovers.
- Leftovers are best stored in an airtight container for up to five days. Mozzarella balls are best placed back in their original container with the liquid they came in.
- The exact quantities of ingredients may vary based on the side of the board used.
- These ingredients can be placed in any order you like, just alternate between white ingredients and red ingredients to create a candy cane effect.
- Use a toothpick to secure the folded pieces of salami if you like.
- Some alternative white ingredients include; crackers, sliced baguette, feta cheese, baby bell cheese, mini brie cheese, nuts such as macadamia or blanched almonds, white chocolate.
- Some alternative red ingredients include; cherry tomatoes, prosciutto, strawberries, sweet cherry peppers, red candies.

Santa Charcuterie Board

This festive Santa Charcuterie Board is an eye-catching centerpiece for your Christmas appetizer table! Fill it with fresh red and green fruits and white cheese and crackers for a healthy and delicious snack to graze on throughout the day.

PREP TIME: 15 minutes
TOTAL TIME: 15 minutes

EQUIPMENT

- electric hand mixer
- large charcuterie board
- round bowl

INGREDIENTS

- 7 oz marshmallow fluff
- 8 oz whipped cream cheese
- 1 teaspoon vanilla extract
- 1 lb strawberries
- 16 oz mozzarella pearls
- 2 lbs green grapes
- 12 oz raspberries
- 2 cups blueberries
- 5 cranberries
- 12 oz crackers

PATTERN

- Make the fruit dip by blending the marshmallow fluff, whipped cream cheese and vanilla extract with an electric hand blender until smooth, about 1 minute.

- Pour the dip into a round bowl and place at the center of the board as Santa's face. Make the eyes, nose, mouth and cheeks using cranberries and blueberries.

- Arrange the remaining ingredients on the board as pictured, starting with the strawberries as the hat and the mozzarella pearls as the beard. It's easiest to start in the middle and work your way out to the edges.

NUTRITION

- Serving: 5oz
- Calories: 196kcal
- Carbohydrates: 25g
- Protein: 6g
- Fat: 9g
- Saturated Fat: 3g
- Polyunsaturated Fat: 2g
- Monounsaturated Fat: 1g
- Trans Fat: 1g
- Cholesterol: 8mg
- Sodium: 168mg
- Potassium: 179mg
- Fiber: 3g
- Sugar: 12g
- Vitamin A: 46IU
- Vitamin C: 21mg
- Calcium: 121mg
- Iron: 1mg

Grinch Themed Charcuterie Board

This Grinch Christmas Charcuterie Board is perfect for holiday entertaining. It's simple to make and impressive to serve!

PREP TIME: 20 mins
ADDITIONAL TIME: 2 hrs 15 mins
TOTAL TIME: 2 hrs 35 mins

INGREDIENTS

- Salami
- Broccoli
- Cherry tomatoes
- Fresh rosemary
- Grinch Cheeseball + additional ingredients to make face and hat
- Pita crackers
- Star crackers
- Cheddar cheese cubes
- Pepper Jack cheese cubes
- Half of a pretzel rod
- Mild cheddar slices
- Muster cheese slice
- Sausage bites
- Gift shape cookie cutter
- Star shape cookie cutter

INSTRUCTIONS

How to Assemble a Grinch-Themed Charcuterie Board

Prepare the Grinch Cheese Ball

- Make a Grinch Cheeseball and position it with the Santa hat on the board.

Create the Whoville Tree

- Lay the rosemary on the board into the shape of a Whoville tree with it curved at the top. Add a half piece of pretzel rod at the bottom for the trunk. Position broccoli and cherry tomatoes throughout the tree to make it fuller.
- Take a slice of Munster cheese and make a star using the star shaped cookie cutter. Place the cheese star at the end of the Whoville tree.

Fill the Charcuterie Board

- Fill the board with meats, crackers and cheeses until there are no more empty spaces. Add some serving utensils, appetizer plates and enjoy.

NOTES

What to Put on a Charcuterie Board

My Grinch Christmas Charcuterie Board is filled with festive foods, but also leaves room for your own creativity. The best part? You can make them in any shape or size with endless possibilities of ingredient combinations.

Use this list to get an idea of a variety of meats, cheeses, fruits, veggies and dips you can use for your board. Check out the recipe section for creamy dips to turn your board into an unbeatable platter.

- Cured meats: salami, capicola, prosciutto, ham, roast beef.
- Cheeses: cheddar, gouda, brie, mozzarella, pepper jack.
- Fruit and Vegetables: grapes, strawberries, dried fruit, pickles, olives, celery, carrots.
- Breads: mini toast, sliced baguette, rye bread.
- Crackers: club, buttery, wheat, whole grain or water crackers.
- Nuts & Snacks: cashews, pretzels, almonds, pistachios.
- Dips or Spreads: pepper jelly, jam, cheese ball, olive oil, spinach dip.

Vegan Charcuterie Board

Prep Time: 1 hr 30 mins
Total Time: 1 hr 30 mins

Ingredients

- **Dips**
  Baba Ganoush
  Roasted Carrot Hummus
  Sun-Dried Tomato Pate
  Edamame Hummus
  Tomato Chutney
  Vegan Cream Cheese
- **Fresh Fruit**
  Grapes
  Raspberries
  Blueberries
  Cherry Tomatoes
  Cucumber
  Red and Green Apple
  Kiwi
- **Nuts and Dried Fruits**
  Walnuts
  Dried Apricots
  Dates
  Raisins
  Roasted Almonds
  Olives

Instructions

- Make the dips. You can find the recipes for each dip on our website. We left all the links on the post above. Keep them in the fridge until you start making the board.
- Choose the board you will be serving the charcuterie items on. Adjust the board size to the amount of people that this will be served to. Place the pinch bowls where the dips will be served so you know where to start adding the rest of the ingredients.
- Start by adding the fresh fruits. Our board contains blueberries, raspberries, kiwi, cucumber, tomatoes and grapes. We add apple too, but at the end to avoid oxidation. You can add any fruits or veggies you want. Raw carrots, celery sticks, strawberries or blackberries are lovely options too.
- Add the dried fruits and nuts. On our board you will find dried apricots, walnuts, olives, almonds, raisins and dates.
- Fill up the pinch bowls with the dips. We use Baba Ganoush, Sun-Dried Tomato Pâté, Roasted Carrot Hummus, Tomato Chutney, Vegan Cream Cheese and Edamame Hummus.
- Fill the empty spaces with an assortment of crackers and sliced apples. We like using a red and a green apple for colour contrast.

TIPS

- When serving the Charcuterie Board, bring out some extra crackers and bread. Crackers are normally the first items on the board that will go. Have some extra crackers and bread so people can keep enjoying the dips and chutneys.
- Plan ahead. Make the dips the day before and keep them in the fridge using an air-tight container. Buy an assortment of crackers, olives, and dried and fresh fruits to make a colourful and complete board.
- To make the Charcuterie Board fancier, serve different types of your favourite vegan cheese and vegan cold "meat" as well. We want to keep the board simple and on a budget, so we made a simple vegan cream cheese instead.
- Use seasonal ingredients as they will be easier to find and always taste better.
- If you want to save time, use store-bought dips. Nothing tastes better like homemade dips but if you are in a rush, or want to make something really quick without making a mess, just use good quality store-bought dips.

Christmas
Candy
Charcuterie
Board

37

INGREDIENTS

- Milk chocolate flavored Stirring Spoons
- Santa Holiday Party Pals
- Minty Bells
- Rudolph The Red Nosed Reindeer Snack Mix
- Assorted cookies and graham crackers, etc.
- Peppermint buttercream frosting, Nutella, etc.
- Wood cutting board

INSTRUCTIONS

- It is so much fun to assemble this treat board! You can place candy in small dishes.

- Add a little chocolate frosting in the middle of the spoons and topped with mini marshmallows. So cute!

- Have fun arranging your board any way you like! It is fun to mix sweet with savory!

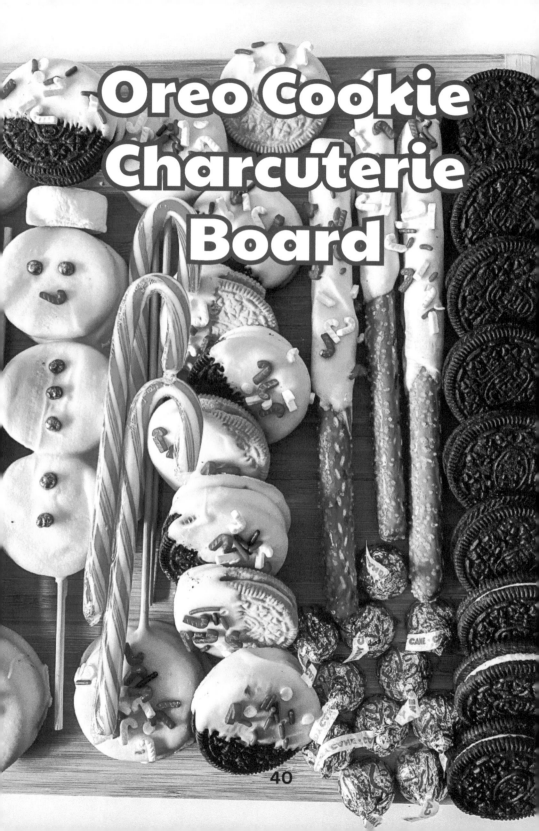

Oreo Cookie Charcuterie Board

Have fun making this kid-friendly holiday Oreo cookie charcuterie board packed with delicious chocolate treats!

PREP TIME: 10 minutes
TOTAL TIME: 10 minutes

Ingredients

- Chocolate Oreo cookies
- Golden Oreo cookies
- Dipped pretzel rods
- Dipped Oreo cookies
- Oreo cookie pops
- Marshmallows
- Hershey's peppermint kisses
- Candy canes

Instructions

- Begin by placing your main items or larger items onto the board. I used the plain and dipped Oreo's on the outside and in lines on the inside of the board.
- Tuck smaller items into the open areas matching flavors together.
- Fill in any gaps with the smallest items, in this case the candy and marshmallows.

Notes

Add or subtract items from the list to create the perfect grazing board for your family.

Ugly Christmas Sweaters Charcuterie Board

Prep time: 45 MINS
Total time: 45 MINS

Ingredients

- 1 3 1/2 lb Fruit cake
- 12 candy canes
- 10 oz Peanut brittle
- 7 oz caramel and cheddar popcorn mix
- 20 Spam and Cheese Skewers
- 12 oz spam
- 12 oz cheese cubes
- 6 oz black olives, pitted
- 8 oz Peppermint bark
- 10 oz Trader Joes english toffee
- 1 c Salted peanuts
- 10 prosciutto cheese rolls
- 4 oz 1 sleeve Trader Joes scalloped crackers
- 1 Jello mold
- 12 Trader Joes chocolate pretzel twists
- 6 Ham and Pickle Skewers
- 6 sweet pickles
- 1/2 cup creme cheese
- 6 slices black forest ham
- 8 oz cheese ball
- 8 pigs in a blanket
- 8 hotdogs
- 1 tube crescent rolls
- ketchup
- yellow mustard
- 1 lb Trader Joes fruit jellies

Instructions

- On a prepared board, place the fruit cake and jello (each on a plate). In small dishes, put the cheese ball, olives, and cherries.
- Make ham and pickle skewers by wrapping the ham around the pickle and cutting into small pieces, threading with a small skewer.
- Make pigs in a blanket with crescent rolls and hot dogs. Cut into bite-size pieces.
- Place 2 small bowls of mustard and ketchup near the pigs in a blanket.
- Fill in the open ares with the remaining foods. ENJOY!

Vegan Charcuterie Christmas Wreath

This vegan Christmas wreath snack board is assembled with fresh rosemary and skewers of vegan deli meat, vegan cheese, tomatoes, peppers, olives, and artichoke hearts. Serve with crackers and hummus for a delicious holiday appetizer.

Prep Time: 15 minutes
Total Time: 15 minutes
Yield: 20 skewers

Ingredients

- 20–25 (4 inch) skewers
- 1 block vegan cheese, cut into 1 inch cubes (I used Daiya Jalapeño Havarti Style Block)
- 1 package vegan deli meat (I used Tofurky Deli Slices)
- 30 pitted olives of choice (I used a mix of kalamata and castelvetrano olives)
- 15 small tomatoes (I used grape tomatoes)
- 15 small peppers of choice (I used peppadew peppers)
- 1 (14oz) can quartered artichoke hearts, rinsed and drained
- 1 bunch fresh rosemary, for garnish
- **Additional ingredients (optional, for serving)**
  + Crackers
  + Hummus

Instructions

- Lay out all of your ingredients for easy skewer assembly.
- To assemble the skewers, choose 5 ingredients and place them on the skewer. Alternate the ingredients and pattern you use for each skewer so your charcuterie board will look more dynamic.
-
- After you assemble a skewer, add it to a large plate or serving platter. Line the skewers up alongside the rim of the plate, forming a circular wreath shape. Add more skewers until you run out of space on your plate.
- Add sprigs of fresh rosemary between the skewers for garnish.
- Enjoy! Serve as is or with crackers and hummus.

Notes

- Feel free to substitute any ingredients and customize this recipe! You can't mess it up.

- For adding the vegan deli meat to the skewer, fold it in half 3-4 times to form a small triangle.

- For best results, use a 10-14 in plate or serving platter for 20-25 skewers.

Nutrition

- Serving Size: 1 skewer
- Calories: 118.3 kcal
- Sugar: 1.2 g
- Sodium: 405.5 mg
- Fat: 7.2 g
- Saturated Fat: 2.8 g
- Unsaturated Fat: 0 g
- Trans Fat: 0 g
- Carbohydrates: 8.7 g
- Fiber: 0.9 g
- Protein: 3.3 g
- Cholesterol: 0 mg

Festive Christmas Charcuterie Board

Prep Time: 16 mins
Total Time: 16 mins

A fun combination of red, white, and green foods to create the ultimate Christmas charcuterie board! This meat and cheese board is quick and easy to assemble, and absolutely perfect for your holiday party.

Ingredients

- 1 (8-ounce) package Cigliegine mozzarella balls
- 1 ½ cup cherry tomatoes, separated
- ⅓ cup basil leaves
- 2 tablespoons balsamic reduction (optional)
- 8 ounce wheel of brie
- 2 tablespoons cherry, raspberry, or strawberry jam
- About 4 sprigs of rosemary, cut into 2-3" pieces (optional)
- 3 cranberries (optional)
- ⅓ cup green olives
- ½ cup garlic-flavored or regular hummus
- ⅓ cup candied pecans
- 4 ounces White Cheddar Cheese, sliced
- 8 ounces sliced salami
- ½ baguette thinly sliced on a bias
- 2 cups green and red grapes, mixed
- ½ English cucumber, thinly sliced on a bias
- ¼ cup sliced radishes
- ½ package (2.5 ounces) water crackers
- ½ package (2.5 ounces) rosemary crackers

Instructions

- The items listed above are merely a suggestion. Feel free to get as creative as you like when it comes to adding to your Christmas Charcuterie Board. Think of the colors you want on your board and find food that matches them, include a variety of textures, and avoid any items that fight with one another flavorwise.

- Have ready a large, round or rectangular serving board or cutting board.

- To make the mozzarella skewers, alternate adding the mozzarella balls, tomatoes, and basil leaves onto a short skewer. Then, stack the skewers on a small plate, and place on the board. Drizzle with balsamic reduction and sprinkle with salt and pepper.

- To assemble the brie, place the brie on the board and spread the jam across the top. Top with small sprigs of rosemary and cranberries, if desired. Place on the board

- Place the olives, hummus, and candied pecans in individual, small bowls and add to the board.

- Then, add in the remaining elements as you'd like, fanning out items like crackers, pears, salami, and cucumber slices. Serve and enjoy!

Kids Christmas Charcuterie Board

Make a 15-minute Christmas Charcuterie Board for kids this Christmas season. Follow the template or use your favorite red, white, and green fruits, vegetables, meats, cheeses, and candies.

PREP TIME: 15 mins
TOTAL TIME: 15 mins
SERVINGS: 10

EQUIPMENT

- charcuterie board
- festive serving bowls

INGREDIENTS

- 1 lb strawberries
- ½ lb raspberries
- 1 package genoa salami
- 1 package pepperoni slices
- 8 oz mozzarella cheese slices
- 8 oz white cheddar cheese cubes
- 1 jar mini dill pickles
- 4 kiwi, sliced
- ½ pint cherry tomatoes
- ½ lb broccoli florets
- ½ cup white chocolate chips
- 1 package m&m's

INSTRUCTIONS

- Arrange serving bowls on your board. Place in opposite corners so they are separated by diagonal lines.
- Arrange foods around the bowls first, then fill in the remaining empty spaces. Keep similar colored foods together.
- Fill the serving bowls with candies and small fruits and veggies.
- Serve immediately.

NOTES

- The ingredients here are suggestions and can be replaced by your favorite seasonal fruits, nuts, cheeses, and meats.
- Calories per serving is based on 8 ounces of a combination of included ingredients, but varies based on chosen foods.

NUTRITION

- Serving: 8oz
- Calories: 339kcal
- Carbohydrates: 20g
- Protein: 15g
- Fat: 23g
- Saturated Fat: 12g
- Polyunsaturated Fat: 1g
- Monounsaturated Fat: 7g
- Trans Fat: 0.2g
- Cholesterol: 56mg
- Sodium: 537mg
- Potassium: 408mg
- Fiber: 4g
- Sugar: 13g
- Vitamin A: 569IU
- Vitamin C: 82mg
- Calcium: 335mg
- Iron: 1mg

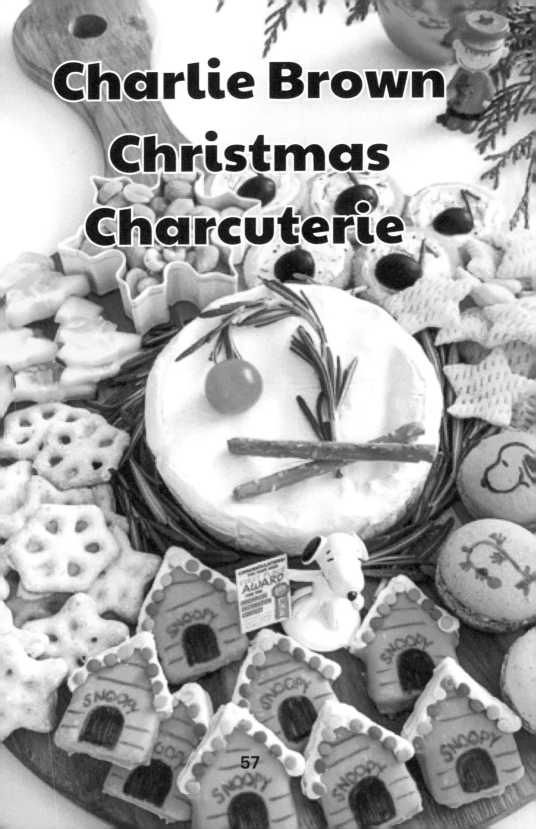

Charlie Brown Christmas Charcuterie

The ultimate Charlie Brown Christmas Charcuterie Board! Perfect snack grazing board for watching the movie A Charlie Brown Christmas!

PREP TIME: 30 minutes
TOTAL TIME: 30 minutes

INGREDIENTS:

- Charcuterie board or serving tray/platter
- Brie cheese
- Fresh rosemary
- 1 cherry tomato
- 2 pretzel sticks
- 1 cucumber
- Mini tree cookie cutter
- Snoopy doghouse Christmas cakes**
- Charlie Brown Christmas macarons**
- Snowflake cookie cutter
- Dry roasted peanuts
- Schroeder's cream cheese & olive dip music note crackers**
- Pop Stars Potato Bites
- Snowflake pretzels

INSTRUCTIONS

- First place the brie in the middle of the board.
- Then place 1 sprig of rosemary in the middle of the cheese and bend it a little to resemble Charlie Brown's tree.
- Next, place the cherry tomato at the end of the tree for the ornament.
- Now place the pretzels stick on the bottom of the rosemary stem in an "x" for the tree stand.
- Arrange more rosemary twigs around the brie cheese so it looks like a little wreath.
- Place the Snoopy Doghouse Christmas cakes on the bottom of the board.
- Now place the Charlie Brown, Snoopy and Christmas Tree macarons on the board.
- Next, slice up some cucumber and using a small tree cookie cutter, cut out tree shapes. Place on board.
- Now arrange Schroder's olive dip music note crackers on the board.
- Then, place a snowflake cookie cutter near the top of the board and fill with peanuts.
- Arrange the Pop Star Potato Bites on the board.
- Finally place the snowflake pretzels on the board.

Individual Christmas Charcuterie Boards

Perfect for entertaining and easy to make with a variety of meat, cheese, and fruit, learn how to make a holiday charcuterie board! These individual charcuterie boards look like ornaments, and look extra festive on a DIY flat Christmas tree!

Prep Time: 15 minutes
Cook Time: 15 minutes
Total Time: 30 minutes
Servings: 8 individual charcuterie boards

INGREDIENTS

- **Pick Two Cheeses**

A firm cheese such as a Manchego.
An aged cheese such as lovely aged sharp Gouda or Cheddar.
A soft and creamy cheese such as Brie, Camembert, or Goat cheese. (A fresh cheese, like burrata or mozzarella, is wonderful, too!)
A blue cheese such as Gorgonzola, Roquefort, or Maytag Blue.

- **Pick Two Meats**

salami/sausages such as soppressata or salame
ham such as prosciutto
deli meat such as mortadella

- **Pick Two Accompaniments**

Crackers
Crisps

Honey or honeycomb
Dried fruit such as apricot and cranberry
Candied Fruits
Olives
Nuts
Sliced fresh fruits or berries
Berries
Grapes

INSTRUCTIONS

- If you use mini boards, embellish them by tying a ribbon around the handle to look like a Christmas ornament. You can also use cocktail plates.
- Begin building your boards by selecting 2 types of meat. I like to select 2 of the following: salami, prosciutto, or soppressata.
- Add 2 kinds of cheese to the boards. Consider Monterey jack, gouda, Manchego, or your favorite cheeses!
- Add 2 accompaniments. In addition to crackers or crisps, add some sweet or savory bites, such as fresh fruit or olives.

Tree Shaped Christmas Cheese Board

This tree-shaped Christmas cheese board is an easy and festive appetizer recipe that will impress your guests and be the centerpiece of your holiday table.

Prep Time: 20 minutes
Total Time: 20 minutes
Servings: 12

Ingredients

- 1 pound assortment of sliced cheese
- 1 pound assorted meats salami, pepperoni, etc.
- 12- ounce box of crackers I used Raincoast Crisps
- 1/2 cup assorted berries
- 1/2 cup sugared cranberries
- fresh rosemary to garnish
- small cookie cutters

Instructions

- Begin creating your holiday/Christmas cheese board by adding two layers of crackers to the bottom of a large cutting board.
- Working upwards, add two layers of sliced cheese. Next, add a layer of sliced meat.
- As you layer, start to form the shape of a tree. (You can use my photos as a reference.)
- Continue layering with more crackers, cheeses, and meats until you reach the top of the tree.
- Decorate your tree with various berries and fruits. Sprinkle with sugared cranberries. Tuck in pieces of fresh rosemary around the tree.
- Using small cookie cutters, cut out shapes from cheese slices. Use the shapes to decorate your tree and board.
- Serve immediately or wrap with plastic and refrigerate until ready to serve.

Printed in the USA
CPSIA information can be obtained
at www.ICGtesting.com
LVHW060712211123
764521LV00018BA/65

* 9 7 9 8 8 6 3 8 4 1 3 0 4 *